TREATS

just great recipes

GENERAL INFORMATION

The level of difficulty of the recipes in this book
is expressed as a number from 1 (simple) to 3 (difficult).

TREATS
just great recipes
fresh pasta

McRae Books

Making Fresh Pasta

All the recipes in this book can be made using fresh pasta bought from a specialty store or supermarket. However, if you would like to make fresh pasta at home follow the instructions on this page.

1

2

3

SERVES 4

PREPARATION 30 min + 30 min to rest

DIFFICULTY level 2

Plain Fresh Pasta

1 Sift the flour and salt into a mound on a clean work surface. Make a hollow in the center and break the eggs into it one by one. Using a fork, gradually mix the eggs into the flour. If making spinach pasta, add the spinach purée now. Continue until all the flour has been incorporated.

2 At a certain point the dough will be too thick to mix with a fork. Use your hands to shape it into a ball. It should be smooth and not too sticky.

3 Knead the dough by pushing downward and forward on the ball of pasta with the heel of your palm. Fold the dough in half, give it a quarter-turn, and repeat the process. Knead for about 10 minutes. Set the kneaded dough aside for 30 minutes to rest.

4 To roll the pasta by hand, flour a clean work surface and place a rolling pin on the top of the ball. Push outward from the center. When the dough is about 1/4 inch (5 mm) thick, curl the far edge of the dough around the pin and gently stretch it as you roll it onto the pin. Unroll and repeat until the dough is almost transparent.

Plain Fresh Pasta
3 cups (450 g) all-purpose (plain) flour
4 large eggs

Whole-Wheat (Wholemeal) Fresh Pasta
2 cups (300 g) all-purpose (plain) flour
1 cups (150 g) whole-wheat
　　(wholemeal) flour
4 large eggs

Spinach Fresh Pasta
2½ cups (375 g) all-purpose (plain) flour
3 large eggs
2 oz (60 g) spinach purée

4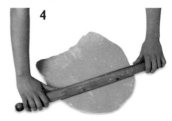

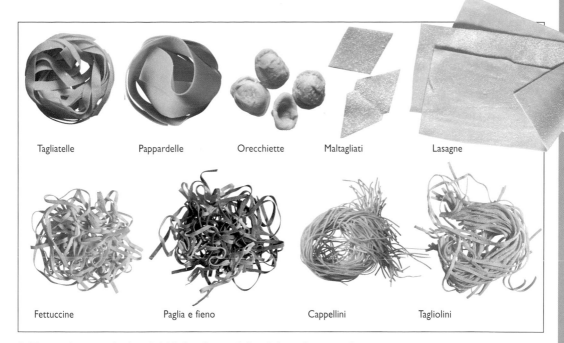

Tagliatelle   Pappardelle   Orecchiette   Maltagliati   Lasagne

Fettuccine   Paglia e fieno   Cappellini   Tagliolini

5 To cut the pasta by hand, fold the sheet of dough loosely into a flat roll. Use a sharp knife to cut the roll into ⅛-in (3-mm) slices for tagliolini, ¼-inch (5-mm) slices for fettuccine, ½-inch (1-cm) slices for tagliatelle, or ¾-inch (2-cm) slices for pappardelle. Unravel the strips of pasta and lay them on a clean cloth. To make lasagna, cut the dough into 3 x 12-inch (8 x 30-cm) sheets. To make maltagliati, roll the dough in strips about 2 inches (5 cm) wide and cut into diamond shapes. Paglia e fieno pasta for 4 servings is made with one half quantity each of plain fettuccine and spinach fettuccine.

6 To roll the dough using a pasta machine, divide it into 4–6 pieces and flatten by hand. Set the machine with its rollers at the widest and run each piece through the machine. Reduce the width by a notch and repeat until all the pasta has been rolled at the thinnest setting. Cut into sheets about 12 inches (30 cm) long. Attach the cutters to the pasta machine and set it at the widths given for the various types of pasta. Lay the cut pasta out on clean cloths to dry for 2 hours before use.

SERVES 4

PREPARATION 20 min + 1 h to make pasta

COOKING 30 min

DIFFICULTY level 2

Tagliatelle
with peas and pancetta

If using homemade pasta, prepare the tagliatelle following the instructions on pages 4–5. • Bring a large pot of salted water to a boil over high heat. • Melt ¼ cup (60 g) of the butter in a large frying pan over medium heat. Add the onion, pancetta, and garlic and sauté until softened, about 5 minutes, • Add the peas and season with salt, pepper, and sugar. • Pour in the water, cover, and simmer for 10 minutes. • Uncover and cook until the sauce has reduced by half, about 10 minutes. • Cook the pasta in the boiling water until al dente, 3–4 minutes. • Drain and add to the sauce. Toss with the remaining butter, Parmesan, and parsley. Serve hot.

14 oz (400 g) storebought or homemade tagliatelle (see pages 4–5)
⅓ cup (90 g) butter
1 onion, finely chopped
½ cup (60 g) diced pancetta (or bacon)
1 clove garlic, finely chopped
2 cups (300 g) frozen peas
Salt and freshly ground white pepper
⅛ teaspoon sugar
2 cups (500 ml) hot water
½ cup (60 g) freshly grated Parmesan
1 tablespoon finely chopped parsley

Paglia e Fieno
with gorgonzola cheese

If using homemade pasta, prepare the paglia e fieno following the instructions on pages 4–5. • Bring a large pot of salted water to a boil over high heat. • Melt the butter in a medium saucepan over low heat and add the Gorgonzola and cream. Season with salt and pepper. Cook over low heat, stirring constantly, until the cheese has melted. • Cook the pasta in the boiling water until al dente, 3–4 minutes. • Drain the pasta and transfer to a heated serving dish. Add the Gorgonzola sauce, tossing carefully with two forks. • Sprinkle with the Parmesan and serve hot.

14 oz (400 g) storebought or homemade paglia e fieno pasta (see pages 4–5)
1/4 cup (60 g) butter
8 oz (250 g) Gorgonzola cheese, cut into small cubes
2/3 cup (150 ml) heavy (double) cream
Salt and freshly ground white pepper
4 tablespoons freshly grated Parmesan

Tagliatelle
with pancetta and radicchio

If using homemade pasta, prepare the tagliatelle following the instructions on pages 4–5. • Bring a large pot of salted water to a boil over high heat. • Melt the butter in a large frying pan over a medium heat. Add the onion and sauté until softened, about 5 minutes. • Add the pancetta and sauté until crisp, about 5 minutes. • Add the radicchio and season with salt and pepper. Pour in the wine and stir until it evaporates, about 10 minutes. • Cook the pasta in the boiling water until al dente, 3–4 minutes. • Drain and add to the pan with the radicchio. Toss carefully and serve hot.

14 oz (400 g) storebought or homemade tagliatelle (see pages 4–5)
Generous $1/3$ cup (100 g) butter
1 red onion, finely chopped
1 cup (125 g) smoked pancetta (or bacon), cut into thin slices
1 lb (500 g) red Treviso radicchio (or chicory), finely shredded
Salt and freshly ground black pepper
1 cup (250 ml) dry red wine

Orecchiette

with turnip greens

Cook the turnip greens in salted boiling water until tender, 12–15 minutes. • Use a slotted spoon to remove the greens, reserving the cooking water. • Heat the oil in a large frying pan over medium heat. Sauté the garlic until pale gold, 2–3 minutes. • Turn the heat down to low and add the anchovies. Stir until they dissolve into the oil, about 5 minutes. • Add the greens and sauté until well mixed, about 5 minutes. Season with salt. • Return the cooking water from the greens to a boil. Add the orecchiette and cook until al dente, about 10 minutes. • Drain and add to the sauce. • Toss well and serve hot.

2 lb (1 kg) turnip greens, coarsely chopped

4 cloves garlic, lightly crushed but whole

1/3 cup (90 ml) extra-virgin olive oil

6 anchovy fillets

1 lb (500 g) fresh storebought orecchiette

Salt

Pappardelle

with beans

If using homemade pasta, prepare the pappardelle following the instructions on pages 4–5. • Place the beans in a large saucepan. Add enough water to cover, the bay leaf, and 2 tablespoons of oil and bring to a boil over low heat. • Simmer until tender, about 1 hour. • Season with salt and cook for 10 minutes more. Drain. If using canned beans, skip this step. • Bring a large pot of salted water to a boil over high heat. • Sauté the garlic and chile peppers in the oil in a small frying pan over medium heat until pale gold, 2–3 minutes. Stir in the beans. • Cook the pasta in the boiling water until al dente, 3–4 minutes. • Drain and add to the pan. Toss well and serve hot.

14 oz (400 g) storebought or homemade pappardelle (see pages 4–5)

12 oz (350 g) fresh cannellini or white kidney beans, rinsed (or one 14-oz/400-g can, drained)

1 bay leaf

Salt

2 cloves garlic, finely chopped

2–3 dried chile peppers, crumbled

1/3 cup (90 ml) extra-virgin olive oil

SERVES 4

PREPARATION 30 min + I h to make pasta

COOKING 2 h 30 min

DIFFICULTY level 2

Pappardelle
with wild boar sauce

If using homemade pasta, prepare the pappardelle following the instructions on pages 4–5. • Heat the oil in a large saucepan over medium-low heat. Add the onion, carrot, celery, and a pinch of salt. Cover and cook for 10 minutes, stirring often. • Add the wild boar and sauté over high heat until lightly browned, 7–8 minutes. Season with salt and pepper. Pour in the wine and cook until it has evaporated, about 5 minutes. • Pour in three-quarters of the stock. Cover and simmer over low heat for 2 hours. Stir often, adding more stock if the sauce dries out. • Cook the pasta in a large pan of salted boiling water until al dente, about 4–5 minutes. • While the pasta is cooking, remove the wild boar meat from the pan and chop finely with a large knife. Return to the pan and add the garlic, sage, and rosemary. Season with salt and pepper. • Drain the pasta and place in a serving dish. Pour the sauce over the top and toss gently. Serve hot.

14 oz (400 g) storebought or homemade
   pappardelle (see pages 4—5)
1/4 cup (60 ml) extra-virgin olive oil
I small onion, finely chopped
I carrot, finely chopped
I stalk celery, finely chopped
Salt and freshly ground black pepper
I lb (500 g) wild boar meat,
   coarsely chopped
3/4 cup (180 ml) dry red wine
I cup (250 ml) beef stock
   (homemade or bouillon cube)
2 cloves garlic, finely chopped
I sprig fresh sage, finely chopped
I sprig fresh rosemary, finely chopped

Maltagliati
with sausages

If using homemade pasta, prepare the maltagliati following the instructions on pages 4–5. • Prick the sausages well with a fork and cook for 3 minutes in a pan of boiling water. Drain, peel, and chop coarsely. • Heat the oil in a large frying pan over low heat and sweat the onion with a pinch of salt for 10 minutes. • Add the chopped sausage meat and sauté over high heat for 5 minutes. • Season with the cinnamon, salt, and pepper. Pour in the wine and cook until it has evaporated, about 5 minutes. • Add the tomatoes and simmer for 20 minutes over low heat. • Cook the pasta in the pan of salted boiling water until al dente, about 4 minutes. • Drain the pasta and add to the pan with the sauce. Toss gently and sprinkle with the Parmesan. • Serve hot.

14 oz (400 g) storebought or homemade maltagliati (see pages 4–5)

4 fresh Italian sausages (about 12 oz/350 g)

2 tablespoons extra-virgin olive oil

1 red onion, finely chopped

Salt and freshly ground black pepper

$\frac{1}{2}$ teaspoon ground cinnamon

$\frac{1}{2}$ cup (125 ml) dry red wine

1 (14-oz/400-g) can tomatoes, with juice

4 tablespoons freshly grated Parmesan

SERVES 4

PREPARATION 30 min + 1 h to make pasta

COOKING 30 min

DIFFICULTY level 2

Maltagliati
with beans and prosciutto

If using homemade pasta, prepare the maltagliati following the instructions on pages 4–5. • Bring a large pot of salted water to a boil over high heat. • Heat ¼ cup (60 ml) of oil in a large frying pan over high heat and sauté the garlic, herbs, and chile pepper for 1 minute. • Add the beans and simmer over medium heat for 5 minutes. Add the tomatoes, season with salt, cover, and simmer for 10 minutes. • Heat the remaining oil in a small pan over high heat. Sauté the prosciutto until crisp, about 5 minutes. Add to the bean sauce. • Bring the water to a boil with the vinegar and a pinch of salt. Add the onion and simmer for 2 minutes. Drain and set aside. • Cook the pasta in the boiling water until al dente, about 4 minutes. • Drain and add to the pan with the sauce. Toss gently, adding the onion and little cooking water if the sauce is too dry. • Serve hot.

- 14 oz (400 g) storebought or homemade maltagliati (see pages 4–5)
- 5 tablespoons extra-virgin olive oil
- 2 cloves garlic, finely chopped
- 2 tablespoons finely chopped fresh herbs (rosemary, sage, thyme)
- 1 dried red chile pepper, crumbled
- 1 lb (500 g) mixed canned beans (cannellini, borlotti, red kidney, white kidney, azuki), drained
- 4 tomatoes, peeled and chopped
- Salt
- 3 oz (90 g) prosciutto (Parma ham), cut in julienne strips (matchsticks)
- 2 cups (500 ml) water
- 5 tablespoons red wine vinegar
- 1 large red onion, sliced

SERVES 4

PREPARATION 30 min + 1 h to make pasta

COOKING 2 h

DIFFICULTY level 2

Pappardelle
with duck sauce

If using homemade pasta, prepare the pappardelle following the instructions on pages 4–5. • Heat in the oil in a large saucepan over low heat. Sauté the onion, bay leaf, sage, carrot, parsley, celery leaves (if using), and ham for 15 minutes. • Add the duck and sauté over high heat until well browned, about 10 minutes. • Pour in the wine and simmer for 15 minutes more. • Stir in the tomatoes and season with salt and pepper. Pour in the stock, cover, and simmer for 1 hour. • Bone the duck and cut the meat into small chunks. Return the meat to the sauce and simmer for 15 minutes. • Cook the pasta in a large pot of salted boiling water until al dente, 3–4 minutes. • Drain and add to the sauce. Sprinkle with Parmesan, toss well, and serve hot.

14 oz (400 g) storebought or homemade pappardelle (see pages 4–5)
1 red onion, finely chopped
1 bay leaf
4 leaves sage, finely chopped
½ carrot, finely chopped
1 tablespoon finely chopped parsley
2 celery leaves, finely chopped (optional)
3 oz (90 g) ham, chopped
5 tablespoons extra-virgin olive oil
1 duck (about 3 lb/1.5 kg), cleaned and cut in 4 pieces
⅔ cup (150 ml) red wine
1 (14-oz/400-g) can tomatoes, with juice
Salt and freshly ground black pepper
¾ cup (180 ml) beef stock (homemade or bouillon cube)
½ cup (60 g) freshly grated Parmesan

SERVES 4

PREPARATION 15 min + 1 h to make pasta

COOKING 30 min

DIFFICULTY level 2

Tagliatelle
with roasted tomato sauce

If using homemade pasta, prepare the tagliatelle following the instructions on pages 4–5. • Preheat the oven to 400°F (200°C/gas 6). • Cut the tomatoes in half and remove the seeds. Place the tomato shells upside-down on a baking sheet. • Bake until the tomatoes have lost their excess water and the skins are burnt, 20–25 minutes. • Let cool a little then slip off the skins and mash the flesh in a large bowl. • Stir in the garlic, oil, parsley, and salt. • Cook the pasta in a large pot of salted boiling water until al dente, 3–4 minutes. • Drain well and place in a heated serving dish. Add the sauce, toss gently, and serve hot.

14 oz (400 g) storebought or homemade tagliatelle (see pages 4–5)
2 lb (1 kg) firm-ripe tomatoes
2 cloves garlic, finely chopped
1/3 cup (90 ml) extra-virgin olive oil
1 tablespoon finely chopped parsley
Salt

SERVES 4

PREPARATION 25 min + 1 h to make pasta

COOKING 5 min

DIFFICULTY level 2

Tagliatelle
with uncooked tomato sauce

If using homemade pasta, prepare the tagliatelle following the instructions on pages 4–5. • Bring a large pot of salted water to a boil over high heat. • Heat the oil in a small saucepan and add the anchovies. Mash with a fork until dissolved in the oil. Remove from the heat. • Cut the tomatoes in halves or quarters and combine in a bowl with the garlic, parsley, basil, and chile pepper, if using. • Cook the pasta in the boiling water until al dente, 3–4 minutes. • Drain and transfer to a serving bowl. Add the tomato mixture and bocconcini, then pour the flavored oil over the top. Season with salt and pepper. • Toss gently and serve hot.

14 oz (400 g) storebought or homemade tagliatelle (see pages 4–5)
1/4 cup (60 ml) extra-virgin olive oil
4 anchovy fillets
14 oz (400 g) cherry tomatoes
1 clove garlic, finely chopped
1 tablespoon each finely chopped parsley and basil
1 spicy red or green chile pepper (optional)
8 oz (250 g) bocconcini (Mozzarella cheese balls)
Salt and freshly ground black pepper

SERVES 4

PREPARATION 20 min + 1 h to make pasta

COOKING 20 min

DIFFICULTY level 2

Maltagliati
with tomato and fish sauce

If using homemade pasta, prepare the maltagliati following the instructions on pages 4–5. • Bring a large pot of salted water to a boil over high heat. • Place the 1 cup (250 ml) boiling water in a pan large enough to hold the fish. Add the fish and simmer over low heat until tender, 5–10 minutes. • Drain, reserving the cooking water, and reserve crumble the fish. • Heat the oil in a large frying pan over high heat and sauté the garlic and chile pepper for 1 minute. • Pour in the wine and cook until evaporated. • Add the fish and tomatoes and cook over high heat for 2–3 minutes without stirring, but shaking the pan frequently. Season with salt. Remove from the heat and stir in the parsley. • Cook the pasta in the boiling water until al dente, about 4 minutes. • Drain and add to the pan with the sauce. Toss gently and serve hot.

14 oz (400 g) storebought or homemade maltagliati (see pages 4—5)
1 cup (250 ml) boiling water
1 lb (500 g) gurnard fillets or other tasty, white-fleshed fish, cleaned
1/4 cup (60 ml) extra-virgin olive oil
2 cloves garlic, finely chopped
1 dried chile pepper, crumbled
1/4 cup (60 ml) dry white wine
4 tomatoes (about 8 oz/250 g), peeled and seeds removed
Salt
1 tablespoon finely chopped parsley

Maltagliati
with sweet walnut pesto

If using homemade pasta, prepare the maltagliati following the instructions on pages 4–5. • Bring a large pot of salted water to a boil over high heat. • Blanch the walnuts in boiling water for 1 minute. Drain and transfer to a large clean kitchen towel. Fold the towel over the nuts and rub them to remove the thin inner skins. • Place the nuts with the sugar, liqueur, chocolate, bread crumbs, lemon zest, and cinnamon in the bowl of a food processor and chop until smooth. • Cook the pasta in the boiling water until al dente, about 4 minutes. • Drain and transfer to a serving dish. Pour the sauce over the top, toss gently, and serve hot or at room temperature.

14 oz (400 g) storebought or homemade maltagliati (see pages 4–5)
¾ cup (100 g) walnuts
½ cup (100 g) sugar
¼ cup (60 ml) Alchermes liqueur or dark rum
1½ oz (45 g) semisweet chocolate, coarsely chopped
1 tablespoon fine dry bread crumbs
Grated zest of ½ lemon
¼ teaspoon ground cinnamon

Tagliatelle
with cream and ham

If using homemade pasta, prepare the tagliatelle following the instructions on pages 4–5. • Bring a large pot of salted water to a boil over high heat. • Melt the butter in a large frying pan over medium heat. Add the ham and sauté until crisp, about 5 minutes. • Pour in the cream and simmer until thickened, about 5 minutes. • Season with salt, pepper, and nutmeg. (The ham will already have flavored the sauce.) • Cook the pasta in the boiling water until al dente, 3–4 minutes. • Drain and add to the pan with the sauce. Simmer and toss gently until the pasta is well flavored with the sauce. • Sprinkle with the Parmesan and serve hot.

14 oz (400 g) storebought or homemade tagliatelle (see pages 4–5)
4 oz (125 g) ham, cut into thin strips
1/4 cup (60 g) butter
Generous 3/4 cup (200 g) heavy (double) cream
Salt and freshly ground white pepper
1/8 teaspoon freshly grated nutmeg
1/2 cup (60 g) freshly grated Parmesan

SERVES 4

PREPARATION 30 min + 1 h to make pasta

COOKING 1 h 30 min

DIFFICULTY level 2

Fettuccine,
roman-style

If using homemade pasta, prepare the fettuccine or tagliatelle following the instructions on pages 4–5. • Heat the oil in a large saucepan over medium heat. Add the onion, carrot, and celery and sauté until the onion is lightly browned, 6–8 minutes. • Stir in the beef and sauté until browned all over, about 5–7 minutes. • Pour in the wine and cook until it has evaporated, about 4 minutes. • Add the chicken livers and cook over low heat for 15 minutes. • Add the tomatoes, mushrooms, and bay leaf and season with salt and pepper. Cover and simmer over low heat for about 1 hour. Remove the bay leaf. • Cook the pasta in a large pot of salted boiling water until al dente, 3–4 minutes. • Drain and add to the sauce. Sprinkle with the Parmesan and dot with the butter. Toss well and serve hot.

14 oz (400 g) storebought or homemade fettuccine or tagliatelle (see pages 4–5)
1 red onion, finely chopped
1 small carrot, finely chopped
1 small stalk celery, finely chopped
1/4 cup (60 ml) extra-virgin olive oil
8 oz (250 g) lean ground (minced) beef
1/3 cup (90 ml) dry red wine
4 oz (125 g) chicken livers, trimmed and diced
1 1/4 cups (310 g) tomato passata (sieved tomatoes)
1/2 oz (15 g) dried porcini mushrooms, soaked in warm water for 15 minutes and finely chopped
1 bay leaf
Salt and freshly ground black pepper
1 cup (125 g) freshly grated Parmesan
1/4 cup (60 g) butter, cut up

Tagliatelle
with duck and vegetables

If using homemade pasta, prepare the tagliatelle following the instructions on pages 4–5. • Bring a small pan of salted water to a boil and blanch the carrots for 2 minutes. Drain and cool in a bowl of cold water and ice. Separately blanch and cool the leek, celery, and onions in the same way. • Heat the oil in a large frying pan over medium heat and sauté the shallot for 4 minutes. Add the ginger. Pour in half the sherry and cook until evaporated. • Gradually add the mushrooms. Cook for 5 minutes, then stir in the blanched vegetables. Cook for 3 minutes more, then stir in the Swiss chard and half the stock. Cook over high heat for 2 minutes. • Lightly flour the pieces of duck. • Melt the butter in a large frying pan over high heat and sauté the duck for 1 minute. Season with salt and pepper. Pour in the remaining sherry and cook until evaporated. • Add the duck to the vegetables. • Stir the cornstarch into the remaining stock in a small bowl then stir into the sauce. Bring the sauce to a boil, then turn off the heat. • Cook the pasta in a large pan of salted boiling water until al dente, about 3–4 minutes. • Drain the pasta toss with the sauce. • Serve hot.

14 oz (400 g) storebought or homemade tagliatelle (see pages 4–5)
2 small carrots, cut in thin strips
1 leek, cut in thin strips
2 stalks celery, cut in thin strips
2 baby onions, sliced
1/4 cup (60 ml) extra-virgin olive oil
1 shallot, finely chopped
1-inch (2.5-cm) piece fresh ginger root, peeled and finely chopped
1 duck's breast, cut in thin strips
1/2 cup (125 ml) sherry or Vin Santo
6 champignon mushrooms, sliced
1 bunch Swiss chard (silver beet), stalks removed, cut in thin strips
2 cups (500 ml) chicken stock
1 tablespoon cornstarch (cornflour)
2 tablespoons all-purpose (plain) flour
3 tablespoons butter
Salt and freshly ground black pepper

Tagliolini
with almond and basil pesto

If using homemade pasta, prepare the tagliolini following the instructions on pages 4–5. • Bring a large pot of salted water to a boil over high heat. • Chop the almonds, garlic,, and a pinch of salt in a food processor until almost smooth. • Add the basil and tomato and chop until smooth. Season with salt, chile pepper, and the oil. Transfer to a serving dish. • Cook the pasta in the boiling water until al dente, about 2–3 minutes. • Drain and place in the serving dish with the sauce, adding a 2–3 tablepoons of the cooking water if the sauce is too dry. • Toss gently and serve hot.

14 oz (400 g) storebought or homemade tagliolini (see pages 4–5)
4 oz (125 g) peeled almonds, finely chopped
1 clove garlic, finely chopped
Salt
1 large bunch fresh basil
1 large ripe tomato, peeled, seeds removed, and chopped
1 dried chile pepper, crumbled, or ¹⁄₂ teaspoon red pepper flakes
3 tablespoons extra-virgin olive oil

SERVES 4

PREPARATION 40 min + 1 h to make pasta

COOKING 40 min

DIFFICULTY level 2

Pasta Squares
with tomato and pancetta

Pasta Dough: Place the flour, cornmeal, and salt on a clean work surface and make a well in the center. Mix in enough water to make a smooth dough. Knead until smooth and elastic, 15–20 minutes, Shape the dough into a ball, wrap in plastic wrap (cling film), and let rest for 30 minutes. • Roll out the dough to a thickness of $1/8$ inch (3 mm). Cut into $3/4$-inch (2-cm) squares. • Sauce: Sweat the onion and pancetta in the oil in a small frying pan over low heat until the onion has softened, about 10 minutes. • Stir in the tomatoes, season with salt and pepper, and simmer over medium heat for 25 minutes. • Bring a large pot of salted water to a boil over high heat. Cook the pasta in the boiling water until al dente, 4–5 minutes. • Drain and add to the sauce, tossing gently. Sprinkle with the Pecorino and serve hot.

Pasta Dough
2 cups (300 g) all-purpose (plain) flour
$2/3$ cup (100 g) fine polenta (stoneground cornmeal)
$1/4$ teaspoon salt
$2/3$ cup (150 ml) lukewarm water + more as needed

Sauce
1 red onion, finely chopped
5 oz (150 g) pancetta or bacon
2 tablespoons extra-virgin olive oil
$1^1/2$ lb (750 g) tomatoes, peeled and chopped and pressed through a fine mesh strainer (passata)
Salt and freshly ground black pepper
4 tablespoons freshly grated aged Pecorino cheese

SERVES 4

PREPARATION 40 min + 1 h to make pasta

COOKING 30 min

DIFFICULTY level 2

Fresh Pasta

with mussels

Soak the mussels in a large bowl of warm salted water for 1 hour. Pull or scrub off the beards. • Insert a thin knife and twist the knife until the mussels open up. • Pasta Dough: Sift the flour and salt onto a surface and make a well in the center. Mix in the oil and enough water to make a fairly stiff dough. Knead until smooth and elastic, 15–20 minutes. Shape the dough into a ball, wrap in plastic wrap (cling film), and let rest for 30 minutes. • Roll the dough out very thinly on a lightly floured surface. Cut into $1/3$ x 8-inch (1 x 20-cm) strips. • Sauce: Beat the eggs, Pecorino, parsley, chopped garlic, and pepper in a large bowl until well blended. Mix in enough bread crumbs to make a dough-like consistency. • Fill each half of the opened mussels with the filling. • Sauté the whole clove of garlic in the oil in a large frying pan over low heat until pale gold, about 5 minutes. • Discard the garlic. Increase the heat and add the tomatoes. Season with salt and pepper and simmer for 5 minutes. • Add the mussels and cook, covered, over medium heat for about 10 minutes. • Cook the pasta in a large pot of salted boiling water until al dente. • Drain and add to the sauce. Toss gently and serve hot.

2 lb (1 kg) mussels, in shell

Pasta Dough
$1^1/3$ cups (200 g) all-purpose (plain) flour
$1/4$ teaspoon salt
2 tablespoons extra-virgin olive oil
Lukewarm water

Sauce
2 large eggs
2 tablespoons freshly grated Pecorino cheese
2 tablespoons finely chopped parsley
1 clove garlic, finely chopped + 1 clove, lightly crushed but whole
Freshly ground white pepper
$1/4$ cup (30 g) fine dry bread crumbs + more as needed
1 lb (500 g) peeled plum tomatoes, pressed through a fine mesh strainer (passata)
2 tablespoons extra-virgin olive oil
Salt

SERVES 4

PREPARATION 20 min

COOKING 30 min

DIFFICULTY level 1

Orecchiette
with spicy broccoli sauce

Cook the broccoli in salted boiling water until just tender, 5–7 minutes. • Use a slotted spoon to remove the broccoli, reserving the cooking water. • Sauté the garlic and chile in the oil and lard over low heat until the lard has melted, about 5 minutes. • Increase the heat and add the cherry tomatoes. Sauté for 5 minutes, then add the broccoli. • Return the cooking water from the broccoli to a boil and cook the orecchiette until al dente, about 10 minutes. • Drain and add to the sauce. • Sprinkle with the Parmesan and Pecorino, toss well, and serve hot.

2 lb (1 kg) broccoli, divided into florets
2 cloves garlic, finely chopped
1 fresh red chile pepper, chopped
$2/3$ cup (150 ml) extra-virgin olive oil
$1/2$ cup (125 g) lard or butter, cut up
10–12 small tomatoes, finely sliced
1 lb (500 g) fresh storebought orecchiette
6 tablespoons freshly grated Parmesan
4 tablespoons freshly grated Pecorino

SERVES 4

PREPARATION 30 min + 1 h to make pasta

COOKING 15 min

DIFFICULTY level 2

Fresh Pasta
with lard and tomato sauce

Pasta Dough: Sift the flour and salt onto a work surface and make a well in the center. Mix in the lard and enough water to make a smooth dough. Knead for 15–20 minutes, until smooth and elastic. Shape the dough into a ball, wrap in plastic wrap (cling film), and let rest for 30 minutes. • Sauce: Place the tomatoes and salt in a large saucepan over medium heat with the onion, garlic, basil, oil, sugar, and salt. Cover and bring to a boil over medium heat. Simmer for about 40 minutes, or until the sauce has thickened. • Remove from the heat and run through a food mill or chop in a food processor or blender until smooth. • Roll the dough out and cut in strips. Cut the strips into pieces about 4-inches (10 cm) long. Give each piece a gentle twist. • Lay the pasta on a kitchen cloth dusted with semolina. • Cook the pasta in a large pot of salted boiling water until al dente, about 5 minutes. • Drain and serve hot with the tomato sauce and Pecorino.

Pasta Dough
2⅔ cups (400 g) all-purpose (plain) flour
¼ teaspoon salt
1 tablespoon lard, chopped
Lukewarm water

Sauce
3 lb (1.5 kg) firm-ripe tomatoes, peeled and coarsely chopped
Salt
1 red onion, thinly sliced
2 cloves garlic, finely chopped
Leaves from 1 small bunch basil, torn
2 tablespoons extra-virgin olive oil
½ teaspoon sugar
½ cup (60 g) freshly grated Pecorino cheese

Rustic Tagliatelle

Heat the oil in a large frying pan over high heat. Add the onion, celery, and carrot and sauté for 5 minutes. • Add the beef and sauté until browned. • Add the mushrooms and parsley and cook for 3 minutes. • Stir in the flour, letting it soak up the oil. • Pour in the wine and cook until evaporated. • Add the tomatoes and season with salt and pepper. Cover and simmer over low heat, stirring occasionally, until the meat is tender, about 1 hour. • Pasta Dough: Sift the flour onto a work surface and make a well in the center. Use a wooden spoon to stir in the eggs, herbs, sausage meat, Parmesan, and enough wine to make a smooth dough. Shape the dough into a ball, wrap in plastic wrap (cling film) and let rest for 30 minutes. • Roll the dough through a pasta machine one notch at a time down to the thinnest setting. Place on a clean cloth and let rest for 30 minutes. • Cut into 1/2-inch (1-cm) wide strips. • Cook in a large pan of salted water until al dente, about 4–5 minutes. • Drain and add to the sauce. Serve hot.

Sauce
1/4 cup (60 ml) extra-virgin olive oil
1 large red onion, finely chopped
1 stalk celery, finely chopped
1 carrot, finely chopped
14 oz (400 g) stew beef, cut into large chunks
1/2 oz (15 g) dried porcini mushrooms, soaked in warm water, drained, and finely chopped
1 tablespoon finely chopped fresh parsley
1 tablespoon all-purpose/plain flour
1/2 cup (125 ml) dry white wine
14 oz (400 g) tomatoes, peeled, and coarsely chopped
Salt and freshly ground black pepper
Water (optional)

Pasta Dough
2 2/3 cups (400 g) all-purpose (plain) flour
2 eggs
2 oz (60 g) herbs (parsley, thyme, basil, mint, etc.), boiled, squeezed dry, and finely chopped
1 tablespoon crumbled Italian sausage meat
1 tablespoon freshly grated Parmesan
1/4 cup (60 ml) dry white wine + more as needed

SERVES 4

PREPARATION 45 min + 1 h to make pasta

COOKING 30 min

DIFFICULTY level 2

Spicy Tagliatelle
with creamy eggplant sauce

Prepare the tagliatelle following the instructions on pages 4–5, adding the chile pepper and thyme to the egg yolks. • Sauce: Boil the eggplants in lightly salted water for 4 minutes. Drain, squeezing out excess moisture. • Heat the oil in a large frying pan over medium heat. Add the garlic and thyme and sauté for 2 minutes. • Add the eggplant and cook for 6–7 minutes, mashing gently with a fork. • Remove from the heat, add half the basil, and season with salt and pepper. Chop in a food processor until smooth. • Return the eggplant cream to the pan and add the tomato. Cook until the tomatoes have broken down and the sauce is creamy. • Cook the pasta in a large pan of salted boiling water until al dente, 3–4 minutes. • Drain the pasta and add to the pan with the sauce. Add 2–3 tablespoons of cooking water, sprinkle with the cheese and remaining basil, and toss gently. • Serve hot.

Pasta Dough

14 oz (400 g) homemade tagliatelle (see pages 4–5)

2 dried chile peppers, crumbled

1 teaspoon finely chopped fresh thyme

Sauce

3 medium eggplants (aubergines,) peeled and chopped into small cubes

$^1/_3$ cup (90 ml) extra-virgin olive oil

2 cloves garlic, finely chopped

1 tablespoon finely chopped thyme

15 leaves fresh basil, torn

Salt and freshly ground white pepper

3 ripe tomatoes, peeled and chopped

6 tablespoons freshly grated Pecorino romano cheese

SERVES 4–6

PREPARATION 20 min + 1 h to make pasta

COOKING 1 h

DIFFICULTY level 2

Baked Pasta
with quails' eggs

If using homemade pasta, prepare the paglia e fieno following the instructions on pages 4–5. • Cheese sauce: Melt the butter in a saucepan. Add the flour and stir to form a smooth paste. Cook, stirring, for 1 minute. • Pour in the stock, whisking to prevent clumps from forming. Bring to a boil and cook over low heat for 20 minutes, stirring occasionally. • Let cool and stir in the Parmesan, Swiss cheese, and cream. Season with salt, pepper, and nutmeg. • Topping: Melt the butter in a large frying pan. Add the vegetables and water and cook over low heat for 10 minutes, until the vegetables are tender-crunchy. Season with salt and pepper and remove from the heat. • Cook the pasta in a large pot of salted boiling water for half the time indicated on the package. Drain and cool under cold running water. • Toss with the vegetables and the cheese sauce. • Preheat the oven to 400°F (200°C/gas 6). • Butter a large baking dish. • Using a large fork, make 4–6 nests of tagliatelle. Arrange them in the prepared baking dish and break an egg into the center of each nest. Season with salt and pepper. • Sprinkle with Parmesan and bake for 15–20 minutes, or until the eggs are cooked. • Arrange the nests in dishes and serve piping hot.

14 oz (400 g) storebought or homemade paglia e fieno or tagliatelle (see pages 4–5)

Cheese Sauce
3 tablespoons butter
3 tablespoons flour
2 cups (500 ml) beef stock
2 tablespoons freshly grated Parmesan
2 tablespoons coarsely grated Emmental (Swiss) cheese
1/4 cup (60 ml) heavy (double) cream
Salt and freshly ground white pepper
1/8 teaspoon freshly ground nutmeg

Topping
3 tablespoons butter
1/2 cup (50 g) zucchini (courgettes), chopped
1/2 cup (50 g) carrots, cubed
1/2 cup (50 g) asparagus tips, cut into short lengths
1/2 cup (50 g) white mushrooms, cubed
3 tablespoons water
Salt and freshly ground white pepper
6 quails' eggs
4 tablespoons freshly grated Parmesan

SERVES 4

PREPARATION 30 min + 1 h to make pasta

COOKING 10 min

DIFFICULTY level 2

Tagliatelle
with egg sauce

If using homemade pasta, prepare the tagliatelle following the instructions on pages 4–5. • Beat the egg yolks in a small bowl. Add the anchovies and Mozzarella and mix well. • Cook the pasta in a large pan of salted boiling water until al dente, about 4–5 minutes. • While the pasta is cooking, melt the butter in a large frying pan. • Drain the pasta and add to the pan with the butter. Add 5 tablespoons of cooking water from the pasta pan and the egg mixture and toss gently until the sauce is creamy (the egg should not solidify into hard pieces). • Season with pepper and sprinkle with the Parmesan. • Serve hot.

14 oz (400 g) storebought or homemade tagliatelle (see pages 4–5)
3 large egg yolks
6 anchovy fillets
5 oz (150 g) Mozzarella cheese, cut in $\frac{1}{2}$-inch (1-cm) cubes
5 tablespoons butter
Salt and freshly ground white pepper
4 tablespoons freshly grated Parmesan

Brown Tagliatelle
with sun-dried tomatoes

If using homemade pasta, prepare the tagliatelle following the instructions on pages 4–5. • Bring a large pot of salted water to a boil over high heat. • Sauce: Place the tomatoes in a large bowl with the hot water. Soak for about 15 minutes, or until softened. Drain well and coarsely them chop. • Mix the arugula, tomatoes, garlic, basil, olives, oil, salt, and pepper in a bowl. • Cook the pasta in the boiling water until al dente, 4–5 minutes. • Drain the pasta and transfer to a serving bowl. Add the arugula mixture, toss gently, and serve hot.

14 oz (400 g) storebought or homemade whole-wheat (wholemeal) tagliatelle (see pages 4–5)

12 sun-dried tomatoes

I cup (250 ml) hot water

I bunch arugula (rocket), washed, dried, and coarsely chopped

4 cloves garlic, finely chopped

10–12 leaves fresh basil, torn

4 oz (125 g) black olives, pitted (stoned) and lightly crushed (tasty oven-dried are best)

1/4 cup (60 ml) extra-virgin olive oil

Salt and freshly ground black pepper

SERVES 4

PREPARATION 1 h 30 min

COOKING 30 min

DIFFICULTY level 3

Cavatelli
with spicy tomato sauce

Pasta Dough: Sift the flour and salt onto a work surface and make a well in the center. Mix in enough water to make a smooth dough. Knead for 15–20 minutes, until smooth and elastic. Shape the dough into a ball, wrap in plastic wrap, and let rest for 10 minutes. • Clean the board and roll out logs about ²⁄₃ inch (1.5 cm) in diameter. • Cut into ³⁄₄-inch (2-cm) lengths and use two fingertips to push down and turn, hollowing them out into a curved shell. Keep your hands and the pastry board well floured all the time. • Sauce: Sauté the garlic, chile, and bell peppers in the oil in a large frying pan over medium heat for 2 minutes, until the garlic is pale gold. • Stir in the tomatoes and cook over high heat for 5 minutes, or until the tomatoes have broken down. Season with salt and remove from the heat. • Cook the pasta in a large pot of salted boiling water until al dente. • Drain and add to the sauce. Cook over high heat for 1 minute until the sauce sticks to the pasta. Sprinkle with parsley and Parmesan.

Pasta Dough
2²⁄₃ cups (400 g) all-purpose (plain) flour
¹⁄₄ teaspoon salt
About ²⁄₃ cup (150 ml) water, boiling

Sauce
2 cloves garlic, finely chopped
1 fresh chile pepper, finely chopped
12 oz (300 g) green bell peppers (capsicums), seeded and coarsely chopped
¹⁄₃ cup (90 ml) extra-virgin olive oil
2 lb (1 kg) firm-ripe tomatoes, peeled and coarsely chopped
Salt
1 tablespoon finely chopped parsley
³⁄₄ cup (90 g) freshly grated Parmesan

Saffron Pappardelle
with lamb sauce

Prepare the pasta dough following the instructions on pages 4–5, adding the saffron and water mixture to the eggs. Wrap the dough in plastic wrap (cling film) and let rest for 30 minutes. • Divide the dough into 6 pieces. Roll it through the machine one notch at a time down to the thinnest setting. • Use a knife to cut into pappardelle about 5 x ¾ inches (12 x 2 cm). Let dry on a lightly floured cloth for 30 minutes. • Sauce: Heat the oil and butter in a large casserole or saucepan over high heat and sauté the lamb until browned all over. • Pour in the wine or sherry and cook until evaporated. • Season with salt and pepper, lower the heat, and cook for 1 hour, or until very tender, adding enough stock to keep the sauce moist. • Take the lamb out of the pan and remove the meat from the bone. Cut the meat into small strips. • Add 3 tablespoons of stock to the pan with the cooking juices. Add the onion and simmer for 5 minutes. • Add the lamb and cook for 3–5 minutes more. Stir in the flour and 2 cups (500 ml) of stock. Add the lettuce, marjoram, and saffron and season with salt and pepper. Cook over low heat until the lettuce has wilted and the sauce has thickened, about 5 minutes. • About 5 minutes before the sauce is ready, cook the pappardelle in a large pan of salted boiling water until al dente, about 4–5 minutes. Drain well and transfer to a heated serving dish. Spoon the sauce over the top and toss gently. • Serve hot.

Pasta Dough

3⅓ cups (500 g) all-purpose (plain) flour

4 very fresh large eggs + 2 very fresh large egg yolks

1 teaspoon ground saffron, dissolved in 1 tablespoon warm water

Pinch of ground saffron (for the cooking water)

Sauce

¼ cup (60 ml) extra-virgin olive oil

3 tablespoons butter

1 leg of lamb, weighing about 2½ lb (1.2 kg)

½ cup (125 ml) Vin Santo or sherry

Salt and freshly ground white pepper

4 cups (1 liter) beef stock

1 small onion, finely chopped

2 tablespoons all-purpose (plain) flour

1 lettuce heart, cut in strips

1 tablespoon finely chopped marjoram

6–8 threads saffron, crumbled

SERVES 4

PREPARATION 30 min +1 h to make pasta

COOKING 45 min

DIFFICULTY level 2

Milk Pasta

with cherry tomatoes

Prepare the pasta dough following the instructions on pages 4–5, using both flours, the oil, and enough milk to obtain a fairly firm dough. Knead for 15 minutes, then wrap in plastic wrap (cling film) and let rest for 30 minutes. • Divide the dough into 4 pieces and roll them through a pasta machine one notch at a time down to the second thinnest setting. Cut into 1-inch (3-cm) squares. Dry the sheets of pasta on a lightly floured cloth for 30 minutes. • Sauce: Preheat the oven to 350°F (180°C/gas 4). • Cut the cherry tomatoes in half. • Mix the bread crumbs, garlic, parsley, oregano, and half the basil in a small bowl. Add the sugar and half the oil. • Place the tomatoes in a large, shallow baking dish, cut-side up. Sprinkle with salt and the herb mixture and bake in the oven for 40 minutes. • Cook the pasta in a large pan of salted boiling water until al dente, about 4–5 minutes. • Drain the pasta and place in a heated serving dish. Spoon the tomatoes and their cooking liquid over the top. Drizzle with the remaining oil and sprinkle with the remaining basil and a generous grinding of pepper. Toss gently. • Serve hot.

Pasta Dough
1 1/3 cups (200 g) all-purpose (plain) flour
1 1/3 cups (200 g) durum wheat flour
1 tablespoon extra-virgin olive oil
About 3/4 cup (180 ml) warm milk

Sauce
1 1/2 lb (750 g) cherry tomatoes
4 tablespoons fine dry bread crumbs
3 cloves garlic, finely chopped
2 tablespoons finely chopped parsley
1 tablespoon finely chopped oregano
8 leaves fresh basil, torn
Pinch of sugar
1/3 cup (90 ml) extra-virgin olive oil
salt and freshly ground black pepper

SERVES 4

PREPARATION 25 min + 1 h to make pasta

COOKING 4–5 min

DIFFICULTY level 2

Tagliatelle
with tuna, capers, and lemon

If using homemade pasta, prepare the tagliatelle following the instructions on pages 4–5. • Sauce: Place the tuna in a medium bowl and mash with a fork. Add the capers, parsley, mint, garlic, lemon juice, and $1/4$ cup (60 ml) of oil and mix well. Set aside. • Cook the pasta in a large pan of salted boiling water until al dente, 4–5 minutes. • Drain well and place in a large bowl of cold water with the coarse sea salt and the remaining oil. Leave until cold. • Drain well and place in a large bowl. Add the tuna sauce, season with salt and pepper, and toss gently. • Refrigerate for at least 15 minutes before serving. Do not store in the refrigerator for more than 12 hours, as the delicate flavors of the pasta will spoil.

14 oz (400 g) storebought or homemade tagliatelle (see pages 4–5)
14 oz (400 g) tuna preserved in olive oil, drained
$2^{1}/_{2}$ oz (75 g) capers preserved in salt, rinsed and finely chopped
2 tablespoons finely chopped parsley
1 tablespoon finely chopped mint
$1/2$ clove garlic, finely chopped
Juice of 1 lemon
$1/3$ cup (90 ml) extra-virgin olive oil
1 tablespoon coarse sea salt
Salt and freshly ground black pepper

SERVES 4

PREPARATION 45 min + 1 h to make pasta

COOKING 15 min

DIFFICULTY level 2

Tagliolini
with scampi and radicchio

If using homemade pasta, prepare the tagliatelle following the instructions on pages 4–5. • Sauce: Peel the prawns and chop coarsely. Remove the flesh from the heads and claws as well. • Melt the butter in a large frying pan and sauté the garlic with the prawn meat from the heads and claws. • Pour in the brandy and cook until evaporated. • Add the tomato and cook for 3 minutes. Add the remaining prawn meat. Season with salt and pepper and cook over low heat for 1–2 minutes. Add the cream and cook until reduced. • Cook the pasta in a large pan of salted boiling water until al dente, about 2 minutes. Drain the pasta and add to the pan with the prawns. • Add the radicchio, toss gently, and serve immediately.

14 oz (400 g) storebought or homemade tagliolini (see pages 4–5)

1 lb (500 g) scampi or Dublin Bay prawns

3 tablespoons butter

1 clove garlic, finely chopped

1/4 cup (60 ml) brandy

1 medium tomato, peeled, seeded, and chopped

Salt and freshly ground white pepper

3/4 cup (180 ml) heavy (double) cream

8 oz (250 g) Treviso radicchio, cut in julienne strips (matchsticks)

SERVES 4–6

PREPARATION 30 min + 1 h to make pasta

COOKING 40 min

DIFFICULTY level 2

Tagliatelle
with spicy chicken sauce

If using homemade pasta, prepare the tagliatelle following the instructions on pages 4–5. • Place the chicken into a large bowl and sprinkle with the paprika and curry powder. Season with salt. Mix well using your hands, ensuring that the chicken is evenly coated with the spices. • Heat the oil in a large frying pan over medium heat. Add the carrot, celery, and onion, and sauté until the onions are transparent, 3–4 minutes. • Add the chicken and sauté until browned all over, 5–7 minutes. • Add the wine and let it evaporate. • Add the tomatoes and mix well. Cover and simmer over low heat for 25 minutes. Add a little stock if the sauce dries out. • Stir in the lemon juice and season with salt and pepper. Remove from the heat. • Cook the pasta in a large pot of salted boiling water until al dente, 4–5 minutes. Drain, reserving 2 tablespoons of the cooking liquid. Transfer to the pan with the sauce and toss over high heat for 1 minute. Add the reserved cooking liquid and toss again. Sprinkle with basil and serve.

14 oz (400 g) storebought or homemade tagliatelle (see pages 4–5)
2 large chicken breasts, sliced very thinly
1 tablespoon spicy paprika
1 tablespoon curry powder
Salt
1/4 cup (60 ml) extra-virgin olive oil
1 medium carrot, finely chopped
1 celery stick, finely chopped
1 medium onion, finely chopped
1/2 cup (125 ml) dry white wine
14 oz (400 g) chopped peeled plum tomatoes
1/4 cup (60 ml) vegetable stock
2 tablespoons freshly squeezed lemon juice
Freshly ground black pepper
2 tablespoons coarsely chopped basil

Tagliatelle
with tomatoes and meatballs

If using homemade pasta, prepare the tagliatelle following the instructions on pages 4–5. • Cook the zucchini in a large pot of salted boiling water until tender, 3–5 minutes. Remove from the heat and drain, reserving the cooking liquid. • Blanch the tomatoes in boiling water for 2 minutes. Drain well and peel them. Chop the peeled tomatoes. • Heat 2 tablespoons of the oil in a large frying pan over medium heat. Add the white part of the scallions and sauté until softened, about 5 minutes. • Add the garlic, sage, rosemary, and tomatoes, and season with salt. Mix well and simmer over low heat until the tomatoes have broken down, about 10 minutes. • Add the zucchini and mix well, using the tines of a fork to mash the zucchini. Simmer over low heat until the sauce is thick, about 10 minutes. Remove from the heat. • Mix the meat with the egg, half the bread crumbs, the green part of the scallions, the basil, and parsley in a large bowl. Season with salt and pepper. • Shape the mixture into balls about the size of a small walnut. Roll each meatball in the remaining bread crumbs. • Heat the remaining oil in a large frying pan over medium-high heat. Add the meatballs and sauté until cooked through and lightly browned, 8–10 minutes. Remove from the heat using a slotted spoon. Drain on paper towels. • Return the reserved cooking liquid from the zucchini to a boil in a large pot. Add the pasta and cook until al dente, 4–5 minutes. Drain well. • Transfer to the frying pan with the sauce and toss over high heat for 1 minute. Add the meatballs and mix well. • Serve hot.

14 oz (400 g) storebought or homemade tagliatelle (see pages 4–5)

12 oz (350 g) small zucchini (courgettes), sliced thinly

12 oz (350 g) ripe tomatoes

1/4 cup (60 ml) extra-virgin olive oil.

2 scallions (spring onions), white part and green part sliced separately

2 cloves garlic, finely chopped

4 sage leaves, finely chopped

1 tablespoon finely chopped rosemary

Salt

12 oz (350 g) lean ground (minced) beef

1 large egg, lightly beaten

2 cups (120 g) fresh bread crumbs

2 tablespoons finely chopped basil

2 tablespoons finely chopped parsley

Freshly ground black pepper

Pappardelle
with pumpkin and saffron

If using homemade pasta, prepare the tagliatelle following the instructions on pages 4–5. • Preheat the oven to 375°F (190°C/gas 5). • Blanch the leeks in salted boiling water until tender, about 5 minutes. Drain well and transfer to a blender. Add half the oil, the cream, Parmesan, stock, curry powder, salt, and pepper and chop until smooth. • Arrange the pumpkin on an oiled baking sheet. Drizzle with the remaining oil and season with salt and pepper. Sprinkle with thyme, marjoram, and pine nuts. • Bake until tender, about 15 minutes. • Melt the butter in a large frying pan over medium heat. Add the shallot and sauté until tender, 3–4 minutes. • Add the pumpkin and leek purée. Mix well. • Cook the pasta in a large pot of salted boiling water with the saffron until al dente. Drain well and add to the pan. Toss over high heat for 1 minute. Serve hot.

14 oz (400 g) storebought or homemade pappardelle (see pages 4–5)
3 small leeks, sliced
$\frac{1}{3}$ cup (90 ml) extra-virgin olive oil
$\frac{1}{2}$ cup (125 ml) heavy (double) cream
$\frac{1}{4}$ cup (30 g) freshly grated Parmesan
$\frac{1}{4}$ cup (60 ml) vegetable stock
Pinch of curry powder
Salt and freshly ground black pepper
8 oz (250 g) fresh pumpkin, peeled, seeded, and cut into small cubes
$\frac{1}{2}$ tablespoon finely chopped thyme
$\frac{1}{2}$ tablespoon finely chopped marjoram
Scant $\frac{1}{4}$ cup (30 g) pine nuts
2 tablespoons butter
1 shallot, finely sliced
Pinch of saffron strands

SERVES 4–6

PREPARATION 30 min + 1 h to make pasta

COOKING 50 min

DIFFICULTY level 2

Pappardelle
with sausage and mushrooms

If using homemade pasta, prepare the tagliatelle following the instructions on pages 4–5. • Heat the oil and butter in a large frying pan over medium heat. Add the onion and sauté until softened, about 5 minutes. • Add the sausage and sauté until browned all over, about 5 minutes. • Add the mushrooms. Pour in the wine and let it evaporate. • Add the tomatoes and simmer over low heat until the sauce is thick, about 20 minutes. • Add the sage and season with salt and pepper. • Cook the pasta in a large pot of salted boiling water until al dente. Drain well and add to the pan with the sauce. Sauté for 1 minute over high heat. Sprinkle with Parmesan and serve hot.

14 oz (400 g) storebought or homemade pappardelle (see pages 4–5)

2 tablespoons extra-virgin olive oil

1 tablespoon butter

1 medium onion, finely chopped

12 oz (350 g) Italian pork sausage, skinned, cut into bite-size pieces

1 oz (30 g) dried porcini mushrooms, soaked in warm water for 10 minutes, drained, and chopped

1/4 cup (60 ml) dry white wine

1 (14-oz/400-g) can tomatoes, with juice

2 sage leaves, finely chopped

Salt and freshly ground black pepper

1/4 cup (30 g) freshly grated Parmesan

SERVES 4

PREPARATION 10 min + 1 h to make pasta

COOKING 20 min

DIFFICULTY level 2

Spinach Tagliatelle
with fennel and gorgonzola

If using homemade pasta, prepare the tagliatelle following the instructions on pages 4–5. • Bring a large pot of salted water to a boil over high heat. • Heat 1/4 cup (60 ml) of the oil in a large frying pan over medium heat. Add the shallots and sauté until tender, 3–4 minutes. • Add the fennel and sauté until tender, 8–10 minutes. • Add the wine and let it evaporate. Season with salt and pepper. Remove from the heat. • Chop half the fennel and half the thyme in a blender until smooth. Transfer the purée to a large serving bowl. Add the remaining oil and mix well. • Cook the pasta in the boiling water until al dente, 4–5 minutes. Drain well and add to the bowl with the fennel purée. Add the remaining fennel, the remaining thyme, half the walnuts, and half the Gorgonzola. Mix well. Sprinkle with the remaining Gorgonzola and walnuts, and serve hot.

14 oz (400 g) storebought or homemade spinach tagliatelle (see pages 4–5)
1/3 cup (90 ml) extra-virgin olive oil
2 shallots, finely chopped
2 medium bulbs of fennel, finely sliced
1/4 cup (60 ml) dry white wine
Salt and freshly ground white pepper
2 tablespoons freshly chopped thyme
1/4 cup (25 g) chopped walnuts
4 oz (125 g) Gorgonzola cheese, cut into small cubes

SERVES 4

PREPARATION 15 min + 1 h to make pasta

COOKING 25 min

DIFFICULTY level 2

Tagliatelle
with peas and cream

If using homemade pasta, prepare the tagliatelle following the instructions on pages 4–5. • Heat a large frying pan over medium heat. Add the pancetta and sauté until lightly browned and crisp, 3–4 minutes. Set aside. • Melt the butter in the pan and sauté the onion until it begins to soften, 3–4 minutes. • Add the peas and season with salt. Mix well and simmer over low heat until the vegetables are tender, about 10 minutes. • Add the pancetta and parsley. Season with pepper. • Cook the pasta in a large pan of salted boiling water until al dente, 3–4 minutes. Drain and add to the pan with the cream. Toss well over high heat for 1 minute. Sprinkle with the Parmesan and serve hot.

14 oz (400 g) storebought or homemade tagliatelle (see pages 4–5)
4 oz (125 g) pancetta, cut into ribbons
3 tablespoons butter
1 large onion, chopped
2 cups (300 g) frozen peas
Salt
2 tablespoons freshly chopped parsley
Freshly ground black pepper
1/2 cup (125 ml) heavy (double) cream
1/3 cup (60 g) freshly grated Parmesan

Pappardelle
with tomatoes and herb frittata

If using homemade pasta, prepare the tagliatelle following the instructions on pages 4–5. • Beat the eggs, basil, and parsley in a large bowl. Season with salt and pepper. • Melt a little of the butter in a large frying pan over medium heat. Add enough of the beaten egg mixture to coat the bottom of the pan. Cook until set, 2–3 minutes. Slide the frittata onto a plate and let cool. Repeat until all the egg mixture is cooked. Slice into ribbons. • Heat the oil in a large frying pan over medium heat. Add the onion and garlic and sauté until golden brown, about 6 minutes. • Add the tomatoes and simmer until the tomato begins to break down, about 10 minutes. Season with salt. • Cook the pasta in a large pan of salted boiling water until al dente, 4–5 minutes. • Drain well and add to the pan with the sauce. Add the frittata ribbons and mix gently. Serve hot.

14 oz (400 g) storebought or homemade pappardelle (see pages 4–5)
6 large eggs
3 tablespoons freshly chopped basil
3 tablespoons freshly chopped parsley
salt and freshly ground black pepper
$1/4$ cup (60 g) butter
2 tablespoons extra-virgin olive oil
1 small onion, finely chopped
2 cloves garlic, finely chopped
14 oz (400 g) cherry tomatoes, cut in half

SERVES 4–6

PREPARATION 30 min + 1 h to make pasta

COOKING 2 h 30 min

DIFFICULTY level 3

Lasagne
with meatballs

If using homemade pasta, prepare the lasagne following the instructions on pages 4–5. • Blanch the sheets of lasagne in a large pan of salted boiling water in small batches. Lay the blanched sheets of lasagne out on a clean kitchen cloth. • Sauté the onion and beef in a frying pan with the butter until lightly browned- 7–10 minutes. Season with salt and pepper and add the tomatoes. Simmer over medium-low heat for 1 hour, adding stock gradually to the pan to keep it moist. • Preheat the oven to 350°F (180°C/gas 4). • When the meat is cooked, remove from the pan and chop finely in a food processor. Reserve the sauce. • Transfer the chopped meat to a mixing bowl and add the parsley, egg, and half the Parmesan. Shape the mixture into small meatballs. • Heat the oil in a large frying pan and sauté the meatballs until nicely browned, 8–10 minutes. Drain on paper towels. • Butter an ovenproof dish and cover the bottom with a layer of lasagne, followed by layers of salami, Mozzarella, ham, Parmesan, meatballs, and sauce. Repeat until all the ingredients are in the dish. Finish with a layer of Parmesan. • Bake until golden brown, about 25 minutes. • Let rest for 10 minutes before serving.

14 oz (400 g) storebought or homemade lasagne (see pages 4–5)

1 onion, finely chopped

12 oz (350 g) beef loin, in 1 piece

1/3 cup (90 g) butter

Salt and freshly ground black pepper

1 (14-oz/400-g) can Italian tomatoes, with juice

1/2 cup (125 ml) beef stock (homemade or bouillon cube)

2 tablespoons finely chopped parsley

1 large egg

1 cup (120 g) freshly grated Parmesan cheese

1 cup (250 ml) oil, for frying

Butter for the baking dish

4 oz (125 g) salami, cut in cubes

12 oz (350 g) Mozzarella cheese, cut in small cubes

4 oz (125 g) ham, cut in small cubes

Index

Copyright © 2007 by McRae Books Srl

This English edition first published in 2007

All rights reserved. No part of this book may be reproduced in any form without the prior written permission of the publisher and copyright owner.

Fresh Pasta

was created and produced by McRae Books Srl

Borgo Santa Croce, 8 – Florence (Italy)

info@mcraebooks.com

Publishers: Anne McRae and Marco Nardi

Project Director: Anne McRae

Design: Sara Mathews

Text: Carla Bardi

Editing: Osla Fraser

Photography: Mauro Corsi, Leonardo Pasquinelli, Gianni Petronio, Lorenzo Borri, Stefano Pratesi

Home Economist: Benedetto Rillo

Artbuying: McRae Books

Layouts: Adina Stefania Dragomir

Repro: Fotolito Raf, Florence

ISBN 978-88-89272-83-1

Printed and bound in China

Index

Copyright © 2007 by McRae Books Srl

This English edition first published in 2007

All rights reserved. No part of this book may be reproduced in any form without the prior written permission of the publisher and copyright owner.

Spaghetti

was created and produced by McRae Books Srl

Borgo Santa Croce, 8 – Florence (Italy)

info@mcraebooks.com

Publishers: Anne McRae and Marco Nardi

Project Director: Anne McRae

Design: Sara Mathews

Text: Carla Bardi

Editing: Osla Fraser

Photography: Mauro Corsi, Leonardo Pasquinelli, Gianni Petronio, Lorenzo Borri, Stefano Pratesi

Home Economist: Benedetto Rillo

Artbuying: McRae Books

Layouts: Adina Stefania Dragomir

Repro: Fotolito Raf, Florence

ISBN 978-88-89272-95-4

Printed and bound in China